Girl's Guide to
Basic Knitting

Girl's Guide to
Basic Knitting

Jenny Occleshaw

Contents

Introduction

Learning to knit is a really useful skill to have no matter what your age. Many of us learn to knit from Mum or Gran, and although our tastes may be different to theirs we all secretly apsire to mimic their even tension, marvel at the way they make sense of the most complex pattern and their seeming ability to watch the television and hold a conversation all at the same time. Even the most competent knitter had to start somewhere, and learning to knit to an even tension is something you learn as you go.

I hope the projects in this book will be an inspiration to all of you who would like to start knitting but have worried that it's a skill that might be out of your grasp. Most knitting is made up of two basic stitches – knit and purl, and once you've mastered those, as well as casting on and casting off, there are plenty of things that you can make. I have designed these projects with a beginner in mind. They are mostly simple and hopefully things that you would like to have, or may like to make as gifts for friends and family. If you are new to knitting I suggest starting with a small and simple project and really taking your time. Measuring your tension, if one is specified, may seem pointless but it will ensure that your item will come out the right size. Always use the correct ply of yarn but don't feel you have to stick to the colours that I suggest. You are far more likely to complete a project if you make it in your favourite colour. If you get a little bit stuck, don't despair, wool shops are great for advice or you can always email me for help. Once you have completed a project or two I guarantee you will be hooked on knitting for life. It is great for the soul, really practical and very creative. What better way to spend an afternoon? Maybe you'll get together with some friends and create a knitting circle? I love knitting and am inspired to design by almost everything around me. I hope you will enjoy these projects as much as I enjoyed creating them for you.

Jenny Occleshaw
Drop Stitch Designs

Knitting Abbreviations

Beg: Beginning

Cm: Centimetres

Cont: Continue

In: Inches

Inc: Increase a stitch by knitting into the front and back of the next stitch

K: Knit

K2tog: Knit 2 stitches together

M1: Make 1 stitch by picking up the loop that lies between the two needles and knitting into the back of it. Place the new stitch on the right-hand needle

Moss st

P: Purl

P2tog: Purl 2 stitches together

Patt: Pattern

Psso: Pass slipped stitch over

Rem: Remaining

Rep: Repeat

Sl: Slip

RS: Right Side

St: Stitch(es)

St st: Stocking stitch

Tbl: Through back of loops

Tog: Together

WS: Wrong side

Yfwd: Yarn forward

Yrn: Wind yarn around the needle

Crochet Abbreviations

Ch: Chain

DC: Double Crochet

SS: Slip Stitch

Tr: Treble Crochet

Dtr: Double Treble

Tr Tr: Triple Treble

Making an I-cord

Using 3.75 mm (US 5) double-pointed knitting needles and yarn, cast on 3 sts.

Row 1: *K3 sts, slide sts to the other end of needle, pull yarn firmly behind sts, rep from * until cord is the desired length. Sl 1, K2tog, psso. Cont in this way until 1 st remains. Fasten off.

Squares and Stripes Throw

This is an absolute beginners' knitting project. If you can knit and purl you can make this. It is a useful project, which is cosy and warm, and will look great draped over the arm of a sofa or seat of a cosy armchair, or even at the end of a bed.

Stitches Used
- Cast on
- Cast off
- Knit
- Purl

Measurements
80 x 100 cm (31 x 39 in)
Each square measures 20 x 20 cm (8 x 8 in)

Tension
20 sts and 28 rows to 10 cm (4 in) measured over st st on 4.5 mm (US 7) knitting needles.

Materials
4 x 50 g (2 oz) balls of DK (8 ply) in each of 5 colours. I used shades of Pink, Purple and Cream
Pair of 4.5 mm (US 7) knitting needles
Wool needle, for sewing up

PLAIN SQUARES
Make 16
Using 4.5 mm (US 7) knitting needles and yarn, cast on 40 sts.
Work 8 rows garter st.
Next row (RS): Knit.
Next row: K4, purl to last 4 sts, K4.
Repeat these 2 rows 21 times
Work 8 rows garter st.
Cast off.

STRIPED SQUARE
Make 4
Using 4.5 mm (US 7) knitting needles and yarn, cast on 40 sts.
Work 8 rows garter st.
Next row (RS): Knit.
Next row: K4, purl to last 4 sts, K4.
Rep these 2 rows twice more.
Change to contrast colour and continue in stripe pattern of 6 rows main colour, 6 rows contrast, until 42 rows st st have been worked.
Complete 8 rows garter st in first colour.
Cast off.

To Make Up

Darn in all the loose ends and press the squares flat using a warm iron and a damp cloth. On a flat surface, arrange the squares in a colourscheme that you are happy with, 4 squares wide by 5 squares long. Place the first 2 squares RS together, and using matching yarn, back stitch or mattress stitch the pieces together. Repeat until the first row is complete. Repeat for the second row and then place these two rows together with RS facing and sew together. Pin to keep the seams in place while sewing up. Make small stitches to ensure that the seams are firm; if your rug will get plenty of use you don't want the seams coming undone. Check for any loose ends and darn them in. Press lightly, if needed.

Note: You could easily line this throw with a soft cotton fabric. Just find a piece of fabric 1.5 cm (¾ in) larger all the way around, turn in a 1.5 cm (¾ in) hem, press in place, and then pin the fabric to the throw with WS together and stitch carefully all the way around.

Blackberry Stitch IPod Cover

Once you have completed a few of the simpler projects featuring mainly knit and purl stitches you may well want to try something with a stitch pattern. This small iPod cover is an ideal project and is made using blackberry stitch, which is easy to do. The knitted fabric makes a secure container for your iPod and a fabric lining ensures that there will be no scratches.

Stitches Used

- Cast on
- Cast off
- Knit
- Purl
- P3tog: Purl 3 stitches together
- Inc (specific to blackberry stitch): Knit into the back of the stitch but don't slip the stitch off the needle, then purl into the front of the stitch, but don't slip the stitch off the needle, then knit into the stitch again, this time slipping the stitch off the needle
- K2tog: Knit 2 stitches together
- Yfwd
- Garter st: Knit every row

Measurements

14 cm (5½ in) long

Tension

22.5 sts to 10 cm (4 in) wide worked over blackberry stitch on 3.75 mm (US 5) knitting needles

Materials

1 x 50 g (2 oz) ball pure wool DK (8-ply), Beige
25 g (1 oz) pure wool DK (8-ply), Rust
25 g (1 oz) pure wool DK (8-ply), Dark Brown

Pair of 3.75 mm (US 5) knitting needles
Wool needle, for sewing up
Lining fabric, approximately 16 cm (6¼ in) square
2 cm (¾ in) button
Sewing needle
Polyester sewing thread
Sewing machine (optional, but helpful)

IPOD COVER

Using 3.75 mm (US 5) knitting needles and Dark Brown, cast on 40 sts.
Work 4 rows garter st.
Break off Dark Brown and join in Rust. Work 2 rows garter st.
Break of Rust and join in Beige. Work 2 rows garter st.
Commence blackberry stitch patt as follows:
Row 1 (RS): Purl.
Row 2: K1, *K1, P1, K1, all into same stitch, P3tog, rep from * to last 2 sts, K2.
Row 3: Purl.
Row 4: K1, *P3tog, K1, P1, K1 all into the same st, rep from * to last 2 sts, K2.
Cont in blackberry stitch pattern until work measures 12.5 cm (5 in) from cast-on edge.

Purl 1 row Beige.

Knit 1 row Beige.

Break off Beige and join in Rust. Work 2 rows garter st.

Break off Rust and join in Dark Brown. Work 4 rows garter st. Cast off.

STRAP

Using 3.75 mm (US 5) knitting needles and Dark Brown, cast on 25 sts. Work 2 rows garter st. Break off Dark Brown and join in Rust.

Buttonhole row: K2, yfwd, K2tog, knit to end of row. Break off Rust and join in Dark Brown. Work another 2 rows garter st. Cast off.

To Make Up

Fold piece in half with RS tog. Stitch the long side and bottom edge of the iPod case closed using back stitch or mattress st. Darn in any loose ends and turn the right way out.

Cut the lining 1 cm ($^3/_8$ in) larger than the knitted piece all around. Fold in a hem at the top edge, press, then stitch in place. With RS tog, stitch the lining down the long side and across the base. Trim the seam, but do NOT turn the right way out. Insert the lining into the iPod cover. Use a chopstick or something similar to ensure that it is pushed all the way into the corners. Use matching thread and a sewing needle to stitch the top edge of the knitted cover to the top edge of the lining using a hem stitch or slipstitch.

Attaching the Strap and Button

Stitch the end of the strap without the buttonhole in the middle of the iPod cover at the Rust garter st ridge. On the other side sew the button centrally placed 4 cm (1¾ in) from the cast-off end.

Lavender Bag

This knitted lavender bag is ideal for drawers or to hang in your wardrobe. It would also make a great gift. It is simple to make and very sweet: I often make them as Christmas gifts. Little felt flowers make excellent embellishments and are easily found on-line or in craft shops. If you are new to knitting, make this one of your first projects and you will be very happy with the result.

~~~~~~

Stitches Used

- Cast On
- Cast Off
- Knit
- Purl
- Yfwd
- K2tog

Measurements

11 x 15 cm (4¼ x 6 in)

Tension

26 sts and 34 rows to 10 cm (4 in) of st st measured on 3.75 mm (US 5) knitting needles using DK (8-ply) pure knitting cotton

Measure tension carefully: If you have fewer sts than specified, try knitting the tension square with one size smaller needles. If you have more stitches than specified across the tension square, try using one size larger needles.

Materials

1 x 50 g (2 oz) ball Pale Mauve DK (8-ply) pure knitting cotton (A)
Less than 25 g (1 oz) Dark Purple DK (8-ply) pure knitting cotton (B)

Pair of 3.75 mm (US 5) knitting needles
Wool needle, for sewing up
60 cm (23½ in) of 5 mm (¼ in) wide white satin ribbon
Lavender flowers, to fill
1 x 3 cm (1¼ in) dark purple felt flower

Lavender Bag
Using 3.75 mm (US 5) knitting needles and Pale Mauve, cast on 58 sts.
Beginning with a knit row, work 8 rows st st.
Picot row: K1, *yfwd, K2tog, rep from * to last st, K1.
Beginning with a purl row, work another 17 rows st st.
Eyelet row: K1, *yfwd, K2tog, K1, rep from * to end.
Work 7 rows st st.
Next row: K1A, K1B, repeat from * to end.
Next row: P1A, P1B, rep from * to end.
Repeat last 2 rows once.
Work another 20 rows st st.
Cast off.

TO MAKE UP

Fold knitted piece in half, RS tog. Stitch side and bottom edges together using back stitch.

Turn right way out. Turn picot edge to the inside and pin in place. Slip stitch into place. Thread the ribbon through the eyelet holes commencing at the centre of one side. Stitch the felt flower to the same side on the top edge and in the middle. Fill the bag two-thirds full with lavender. Tie ribbon tightly in a knot and then a bow.

Button Bracelet

This is a project for crafters who like to make their own jewelry. It is a simple, bold and colourful statement piece made using plaited I-cords, which start off as one and branch into three sections before returning back to one cord. A feature button cleverly disguises the joins in the seams. You can customise the length of the bracelet to fit any wrist or alter the thickness of the yarn. Why not knit up a few for friends and family for stocking fillers?

Stitches Used

- Cast On
- Knit
- K2tog
- Sl 1
- Psso

Measurements and Tension

9 cm (3½ in) in diameter
Tension is taut for I-cords

Materials

1 x 50 g (2 oz) ball of Noro Silk Garden (aran weight), pink Note: 1 ball will make several bracelets
2 x 3.75 mm (US 5) double-pointed knitting needles
3 safety pins, for holding stitches
2 x 4 cm (1¾ in) buttons

BRACELET

Using 3.75 mm (US 5) double-pointed knitting needles and Noro Silk Garden, cast on 3 sts. Work an I-cord for 3 cm (1¼ in) (see Making an I-cord).
Next: Leave 2 sts on a safety pin. Using the rem st, K, P, K, P all into same st (4 sts).
Work a 4 st I-cord for 26 cm (10¼ in).
Next row: K2tog, twice.
Next row: K2tog.
Leave rem st on a safety pin.**
Next: Place the 2 rem sts from safety pin on the double-pointed knitting needles. Repeat from * to **.
Repeat with the last stitch.
You will now have three 4-st I-cords, each 26 cm (10¼ in).
Next: Plait (braid) the three strands together, not too tightly. Place the rem 3 sts back on a double-pointed knitting needle and work a 3 st I-cord for 3 cm (1¼ in).
Next row: Sl 1, K2tog, psso.
Fasten off.

To Make Up

Darn in all loose ends. Form the bracelet into a circle. If you have something cylindrical to shape it round such as a small can, use it. Place the 2 x 3 cm (1¼ in) I-cord ends on top of each other to complete the circle. Stitch in place. The buttons cover this section. Put 1 on the back and 1 on the front. Pin through the sewing holes

of the buttons, just to check that you are happy
with the position before you stitch everything
firmly in place through both buttons.
To shorten thee bracelet – Make the I-cords
shorter.

Moss Stitch Cuff

Make this moss stitch knitted cuff for yourself or a friend. It is a quick knit and because you are covering a resin bracelet your work will not go out of shape.

This is a great project for using up odds and ends of yarn.

Stitches Used
- Cast On
- Cast Off
- Knit
- Purl
- Inc

Tension
14 sts to 10 cm (4 in) measured over moss st on 3.25 mm (US 3) knitting needles using DK (8-ply) and bouclé yarn together.

Materials
4 cm (1¾ in) wide x 22 cm (8¾ in) diameter resin open-ended bracelet

1 x 50 g (2 oz) ball of DK (8-ply) pure wool, in your choice of colour

1 x 50 g (2 oz) ball of lightweight bouclé yarn or lightweight mohair such as Kidsilk Haze, in your choice of colour

Pair of 3.25 mm (US 3) knitting needles

Wool needle, for sewing up

KNITTED CUFF
Using 3.25 mm (US 3) knitting needles and both yarns together, cast on 8 sts.

Row 1: K1, P1 to end.

Row 2: Inc in first st, *K1, P1, rep from * to last st, inc in last st (9 sts).

Rep Row 2, inc in first and last st and keeping moss st pattern correct until there are 14 sts. Cont in moss st without further shaping until work measures 18 cm (7 in) from cast-on edge.

Next row: K2tog, moss st to last 2 sts, K2tog. Repeat this row until 8 sts rem.

Cast off.

To Make Up
Starting at one end, fold the two sides in to meet the middle. Stitch a short section closed along the length and then fold the open end down to meet the sides. Using very small stitches, sew to close. Repeat this process at the other end. Slip the knitted piece onto the resin bracelet with the open seam to the inside. Stich the open centre seam closed using mattress st. Darn in any loose ends.

Blue Ice Beanie

This lovely soft beanie is knitted in Sirdar Big Softie, a chunky yarn that knits up quickly. It is knitted on straight needles and has simple decreases to create the crown shaping. You can leave the beanie plain or embellish it with a crocheted flower, if you like. This is a nice and easy project for a beginner.

Stitches Used

- Cast on
- Cast off
- K2, P2 rib
- K2tog
- P2tog
- Sl 1, K1, psso

Measurements

To fit: Ladies head – the beanie has a fair bit of stretch.

Tension

12 sts and 14 rows to 10 cm (4 in) on 7.5 mm knitting needles measured over rib pattern. If you have fewer sts than specified, try knitting the tension square with one size smaller needles. If you have more stitches than specified across the tension square, try using one size larger needles..

Materials

2 x 50 g (2 oz) balls of Sirdar Big Softie shade 335 Blancmange (this is a Super chunky yarn which is un-plied and very soft) .
Pair of 7.5 mm knitting needles
Wool needle, for sewing up

3.5 mm (US A/E) crochet hook and oddments of DK (8-ply) yarn in two shades of blue, for the flower

BEANIE

Using 7.5 mm knitting needles and yarn, cast on 52 sts.

Row 1: *K2, P2, rep from * to end.

Rep this row until work measures 15 cm (6 in) from cast-on edge.

Shape Crown

Decrease row: *K2, P2tog, rep from * to end.

Next row: *K1, P2, rep from * to end.

Next row: *K2tog, P1, rep from * to end.

Next row: *K1, P1, rep from * to end.

Rep this row once.

Next row: *Sl 1, K1, psso, rep from * to end.

Next row: *K2tog, rep from * to last st, K1.

Break off yarn, thread through rem sts, pull up tightly and fasten off.

To Make Up

With RS tog, carefully stitch the centre back seam. Note – it may be easier to do this using a finer yarn of the same shade. Darn in any loose ends. Turn the right way out.

CROCHET FLOWER

Make 1

Centre: Using shade A, make a slip ring.

Round 1: RS. 3ch, 15 tr into ring, pull the end to close the ring, sl st, into top of third ch (16 sts).

Round 2: 4ch, (Ss in the front strand of next tr, 3ch) 15 times, sl st into first of 4ch. Fasten off neatly.

Second round of petals: Join in contrast colour. RS. Working behind second round and into the first round, join in the new colour in the top ch of 3ch, 6ch, working in the back strand of each tr; (sl st in next tr, 5ch) 15 times, sl st in first of 6ch. Fasten off neatly.

Classic Navy Knitted Gloves

These knitted gloves are a good project to tackle once you have completed a few smaller knitted items and built up your knitting confidence. My best tip is to buy quality yarn as it will knit up well, and be soft and lovely to wear – they require just a couple of 50 g (2 oz) balls, so why not invest in some beautiful merino DK (8-ply) yarn and you will be well rewarded with a gorgeous pair of long-wearing, soft gloves that you can be proud to say you made. These gloves are knitted on 2 needles rather than the conventional set of 4. This is to simplify the process. It does create more sewing at the end though, so do try to keep your seams very fine.

Stitches Used

- Cast on
- Cast off
- Knit
- Purl
- K2tog

Measurements

To fit: Woman's hand 18.5 cm (7¼ in) long

Tension

23.5 sts to 10 cm (4 in) in width measured over st st on 3.75 mm (US 5) knitting needles using DK (8-ply) yarn. Check tension carefully – If fewer stitches, use one size smaller needles ie 3.25 mm (US 3). If more stitches use one size larger needles ie 4 mm (US 6).

Note: The tension should be slightly tighter than would be suggested for this yarn as the fabric for the gloves needs to be quite firm.

Materials

2 x 50 g (2 oz) balls of pure wool DK (8-ply) Navy
Less than 25 g (1 oz) of DK (8-ply) Cream, for
    contrast cuff stripe
Pair of 3 mm (US 2½) knitting needles
Pair of 3.75 mm (US 5) knitting needles
Wool needle, for sewing up

RIGHT GLOVE

Using 3 mm (US 2½) knitting needles and Navy, cast on 42 sts.
Row 1: K2, *P1, K1, repeat from * to end of row.
Rep this row another 7 times.
Join in Cream and work 2 rows rib as set.
Break off Cream, rejoin Navy and work another 9 rows rib as set.
Change to 3.75 mm (US 5) knitting needles.
Row 1: Knit.
Row 2: K1, purl to last st, K1.**
Row 3: K22, m1, K1, m1, K19.
Rows 4, 5 and 6: K1, purl to last st, K1.
Row 7: K22, m1, K3, m1, K19.
Rows 8, 9 and 10: K1, purl to last st, K1.
Row 11: K22, m1, K5, m1, K19.

Cont in this manner, inc 2 sts on every fourth row until there are 52 sts.
Work 1 row.

Thumb

Next row: K34, turn.
Next row: K1, P12, turn, cast on 3 sts.
Work 16 rows st st on these 16 sts remembering to knit the first and last st on each purl row.

Shape Top of Thumb

Next row: K1, *K2tog, K1, rep from * to end.
Next row: K1, purl to last st, K1.
Next row: K2tog all across.
Break off yarn, thread through rem sts, pull up tightly and fasten off.
With RS facing, join in yarn and knit up 3 sts from the point where sts were cast on at the base of thumb, knit to end of row (42 sts).
Work 11 rows. On each purl row, knit the first and last st.

First finger

Next row: K27, turn.
Next row: K1, P11, turn and cast on 2 sts.
Work 20 rows st st on these 14 sts.
On each purl row, knit the first and last st.

Shape Top

Next row: K2, *K2tog, K1, rep from * to end of row.
Next row: K1, purl to last st, K1.
Next row: K2tog all across.
Break off yarn, thread through rem sts, pull up tightly and fasten off.

Second finger

With RS facing, join in yarn and knit up 2 sts from the point where sts were cast on at the base of First Finger, K5, turn.
Next row: K1, P11, turn and cast on 2 sts.
Work 2 rows st st on these 14 sts.
On each purl row, knit the first and last st.
Shape top: As for first finger.

Third Finger

With RS facing, join in yarn and knit up 2 sts from the point where sts were cast on at the base of Second Finger, K5, turn.
Next row: K1, P11, turn and cast on 2 sts.
Complete as for first finger.

Fourth Finger

With RS facing, join in yarn and knit up 2 sts from the point where sts were cast on at the base of Third Finger, knit to end.
Next row: K1, purl to last st, K1.
Work 16 rows st st on these 12 sts.
Remember to knit the first and last st on each purl row.

Shape Top

Next row: *K2tog, K1, rep from * to end.
Next row: K1, purl to last st, K1.
Next row: K2tog all across.
Break off yarn, thread through rem sts, pull up tightly and fasten off.

LEFT GLOVE

Work as for Right Glove to **
Row 3: K19, m1, K1, m1, K22.
Rows 4, 5 and 6: St st.
Row 7: K19, m1, K3, m1, K22.
Rows 8, 9 and 19: St st.
Row 11: K19, m1, K5, m1, K22.
Cont in this manner, increasing 2 sts in every 4th row until there are 52 sts.
Work 1 row.

Thumb

Next row: K31, turn and cast on 3 sts.
Next row: K1, P14, K1, turn.
Complete as for Right Glove.
With RS facing, join in yarn and knit up 3 sts from cast-on sts at base of thumb, knit to end (42 sts).
Work 11 rows st st, remembering to knit the first and last st of each purl row.

First Finger

Next row: K27, turn and cast on 2 sts.
Next row: K1, P12, K1, turn.
Complete as for Right Glove.

Second Finger

With RS facing, join in yarn and knit up 2 sts from cast-on sts at base of first finger, K5, turn and cast on 2 sts.
Next row: K1, P12, K1, turn.
Complete as for Right Glove.

Third Finger

With RS facing, join in yarn and knit up 2 sts from cast-on sts at base of Second Finger, K5, turn and cast on 2 sts.
Next row: K1, P12, K1, turn.

Complete as for Right Glove.

Fourth Finger

Work as for Right Glove

To Make Up

Press gloves using a slightly damp cloth and a warm iron. Join finger and thumb seams using a flat seam and very small stitches. Check carefully to ensure that there are no small holes where stitches were cast on. Press seams if needed.

Dear Diary Knitted Journal Cover

Make this knitted journal cover for yourself or as a gift. You can decorate it elaborately or keep it quite simple. If you have younger members of the family they might like to make the decorations using felt flowers and leaves. Just make sure everything is securely stitched in place.

Stitches Used

- Cast on
- Cast off
- Knit
- Purl
- Yfwd
- K2tog

Crochet Stitches Used

- Chain
- Sl st
- dc
- tr

Measurements

To fit an A5 notebook with hard cover

Tension

22 sts and 30 rows to 10 cm (4 in) when worked in st st using 4 mm (US 6) knitting needles, knitted with DK (8-ply) cotton/wool blend

   Check tension carefully: If you have fewer sts than specified, try knitting the tension square with one size smaller needles. If you have more stitches than specified across the tension square, try using one size larger needles.

Materials

Note: I have listed the materials exactly as I have used for the embellishments but you don't need to feel constrained to this idea. Once your main cover piece is knitted you can embellish the front cover in any way you desire.

2 x 50 g balls of Patons cotton DK (8-ply)
Pair of 4 mm (US 6) knitting needles
Pair of 3.25 mm (US 3) double-pointed knitting needles
Wool needle, for sewing up
A5 hardback journal
3.5 mm (US 4/E) crochet hook
Small amounts of Dark Blue, Light Blue, Bright Purple and Aqua DK (8-ply), for crocheted flowers
Small amount of Bright Green DK (8-ply), for leaves
6 x 1 cm (3/8 in) translucent pearl buttons, for flower centre
3 charms, for the leaves
1 m x 1 cm (3/8 in) wide ribbon
Polyester thread and sewing needle

JOURNAL COVER

Using 4 mm (US 6) knitting needles and yarn,
cast on 54 sts.

Work 2 rows garter st.

Row 3: K2, purl to last 2 sts, K2.

Row 4: Knit.

Repeat these 2 rows until work measures
47 cm (18½ in) ending with a knit row.

Work 2 rows garter st.

Cast off.

To Make Up

Press piece lightly, using a damp cloth and a
warm iron.

Place the journal in the centre of the knitted
piece, fold 5.5 cm (generous 2 in) flap over the
front cover and secure with a pin. Do the same

on the back. Your journal is now sandwiched into its cover. Stitch along the folded sections just below the garter st ridges. You will notice that the cover is not tight. This is so that when your notebook is full you will be able to slip the cover off and pop it on a new one. Once all four sections have been stitched you are ready to decorate the front.

FLOWERS
Make 6 in different shades of blue and purple
Centre
Using shade A, and crochet hook, make a slip ring.

Round 1: RS, 3ch, 15 tr into ring, pull the end to close the ring, sl st into top of third ch (16 sts).

Round 2: 4ch, (sl st in the front strand of next tr, 3ch) 15 times, sl st into first of 4ch. Fasten off neatly.

Second round of petals: Join in contrast colour. RS, working behind second round and into the first round, join in the new colour in the top ch of 3ch, 6ch, working in the back strand of each tr; (sl st in next tr, 5ch) 15 times, sl st in first of 6ch. Fasten off neatly.

LEAVES
Make 3
Using 3.25 mm (US 3) knitting needles and Bright Green, cast on 3 sts.
Work an I-cord for 1.5 cm (¾ in)
Row 1 (RS): Knit.
Row 2: Knit.
Row 3: K1, m1, K1, m1, K1.
Row 4 and all even rows: Knit.
Row 5: K2, m1, K1, m1, K2.
Row 7: K3, m1, K1, m1, K3.

Row 9: K4, m1, K1, m1, K4.
Row 11: K5, m1, K1, m1, K5.
Rows 13 and 15: Knit.
Row 17: K5, Sl 2, K1, psso, K5.
Row 19: K4, Sl 2, K1, psso, K4.
Row 21: K3, Sl 2, K1, psso, K3.
Row 23: K2, Sl 2, K1, psso, K2.
Row 25: K1, Sl 2, K1, psso, K1 (3 sts).
Row 27: K1, Sl 2, psso, fasten off.

To Make Up
Sew a silver charm to the top (where the I-cord is) of each leaf.

Arrange the leaves in the lower right-hand corner with the points facing upward, to the left and down in a fan shape.

Sew a button to the centre of each flower. Arrange a group of three flowers opposite the leaves and another group of three flowers in the corner diagonally opposite them. Stitch in position using polyester thread. I found it easiest to do this by sewing through the button. It gives a very neat finish.

To attach the ribbon, fold the ribbon in half and sew to the middle of the front of the journal, stitching in place firmly. You will now be able to wrap it right around the book and tie in a bow.

Flying the Flag Bunting

This knitted bunting is easy to make and will brighten up any room. Use it for parties or to decorate a child's bedroom. I have knitted the bunting in Sirdar Snuggly Baby Bamboo, which comes in a range of beautiful colours and has a lovely sheen. However, any DK (8-ply) yarn or cotton would be fine.

Stitches Used
- Cast on
- Cast off
- Knit
- Purl
- Yfwd
- K2tog

Measurements
Each flag measures 22 x 14 cm (8¾ x 5½ in)

Tension
24 sts and 48 rows to 10 cm (4 in) worked over garter st on 3.75 mm (US 5) knitting needles: If you have fewer sts than specified, try knitting the tension square with one size smaller needles. If you have more stitches than specified across the tension square, try using one size larger needles.

Materials
11 x 50 g (2 oz) balls of Sirday Snuggly Baby Bamboo, each a different colour Note: you will not need the whole ball for each flag
Pair of 3.75 mm (US 5) knitting needles
Wool needle
2 m (2 yd) x 1 cm (³/8 in) wide ribbon
22 small buttons
Sewing needle and polyester thread

FLAGS
Make 11 flags, 1 in each shade
Using 3.75 mm (US 5) knitting needles and first colour, cast on 42 sts.
Work 4 rows st st.
Picot edging: K1, *yfwd, K2tog, rep from * to last st, K1.
Beg with a purl row, work another 4 rows st st.
Work 3 rows garter st.
Next row: K2tog, knit to last 2 sts, K2tog.
Rep these 4 rows until 2 sts rem.
K2tog. Fasten off.

To Make Up
Fold them over at the picot edge and stitch to just above where the garter stitch ridges begin. Darn in all loose ends. Thread flags on to the ribbon, spacing them evenly. Stitch a button to the outer edge of each flag and through the ribbon so that each stays in place. Fold back each end of the ribbon to the wrong side to create a small loop for hanging. Stitch in place.

Headband with Floppy Bow

This 1950s-style headband has a gorgeous knitted floppy bow. Knit it for yourself or as a gift. This is a good project to begin practising knitting 'in the round'. Who needs a hat when you can wear this bow?

~~~~~~

Stitches Used
- Cast on
- Cast off
- Knit
- Purl

Measurements
7 cm (2¾ in) wide and to fit an average head size
Bow is 18 cm (7 in) long x 8 cm (3¼ in) wide

Materials
4 x 4 mm (US 6) double-pointed knitting needles
Pair of 4 mm (US 6) knitting needles
1 x 50 g (2 oz) ball of Noro Silk Garden, aran weight, shade of your choice

Tension
22 sts and 28 rows measured over moss st on 4 mm (US 6) knitting needles. Please measure tension carefully as it will affect the size of your headband. If you have fewer sts than specified, try knitting the tension square with one size smaller needles. If you have more stitches than specified across the tension square, try using one size larger needles.

HEADBAND
Using 4 x 4 mm (US 6) double-pointed knitting needles and yarn, cast on 90 sts (30, 30, 30). Join into a ring, being careful not to twist sts.
Round 1: *K1, P1, rep from * to end of round.
Round 2: *P1, K1, rep from * to end of round.
This forms the moss st pattern. Cont in moss stitch until work measures 8 cm (2¾ in) from beg.
Next round: Cast off 84 sts.
Cont on rem 6 sts in moss st as set, working backward and forward in rows until this piece measures 10 cm (4 in) from where stitches were cast off. (This piece is the centre of the bow). Cast off rem 6 sts.

BOW
Using 4 mm (US 6) knitting needles and yarn, cast on 30 sts.
Row 1: *K1, P1, rep from * to end.
Rep this row until work measures 15 cm (6 in) from cast-on edge. Cast off.

To Make Up
Darn in all loose ends. Arrange the bow on the front of the headband. Next, bring the strip of 6 sts and wrap it tightly around the centre of the bow, forming a pleat in the centre. Stitch firmly

in place. A couple of additional stitches at the back of the bow will help keep it in an upright position.

Bobble Knitted Cuff

This knitted cuff is quick to make and is a stylish addition to your wardrobe, or an original and personalised gift. It is a good way of using up oddments of yarn and up-cycling resin bracelets that you no longer wear.

Stitches Used
- Cast on
- Cast off
- Knit
- Purl
- Slip 1
- K2tog
- MB (Make bobble) as follows: K1, P1, K1, P1, K1 all into next st (5 sts). Turn and purl all sts. Turn and knit all sts. Turn and purl all sts. Turn and knit all sts. *Slip second st on needle over the first. Repeat from * until 1 st remains. Cont with patt.
- Inc

Measurements
4 x 22 cm (2¾ x 8¾ in) circumference open-ended bracelet

Materials
1 x 50 g (2 oz) ball DK (8-ply) pure wool Dark Grey
Small amount Rowan Kidsilk Haze Dark Grey
Pair of 3.25 mm (US 3) knitting needles
4 x 22 cm (8¾ in) circumference open-ended resin bracelet
Wool needle, for sewing up

Tension
16 sts and 2 rows to 10 cm (4 in) of knitted fabric on 3.25 mm (US 3) knitting needles using DK (8-ply) and Kidsilk Haze knitted together. If you have fewer sts than specified, try knitting the tension square with one size smaller needles. If you have more stitches than specified across the tension square, try using one size larger needles.

KNITTED CUFF
Using 3.25 mm (US 3) knitting needles, and using both yarns together, cast on 7 sts. Knit 1 row.
Next row: Inc in first st, purl to last st, inc in last st (9 sts).
Repeat these 2 rows until there are 15 sts.
Knit 2 rows.
*Work 4 rows st st.
Next row: K7, MB, K7.
Work 4 rows st st**
Repeat from * to **, 3 times.
Work another 4 rows st st.
Dec 1 st at each end of every row by K2tog until 7 sts rem.
Cast off.

To Make Up

Starting at one end, fold the two sides in to meet in the middle. Stitch a short section closed along the length and then fold the open end down to meet the sides. Using very small stitches, sew to close. Repeat this process at the other end. Both ends are now stitched closed with the middle section open. Slip the knitted piece onto the resin bracelet with the open seam to the inside. Stich the open centre seam closed using mattress st. Darn in any loose ends.

Moody Blues Cowl

This may be the simplest wearable garment you ever knit; it looks amazing and is soft and warm. Once you've knitted one you'll be making them for all your friends as gifts. They knit up quickly on big needles and drape beautifully, adding style to your autumn and winter outfits.

~~~~~~

Stitches Used
- Cast on
- Cast off
- Knit
- Purl

Measurements
80 x 30 cm (31 x 12 in)

Tension
9 sts and 13 rows to 10 cm (4 in) on 7.5 mm knitting needles measured over moss st. If you have fewer sts than specified, try knitting the tension square with one size smaller needles. If you have more stitches than specified across the tension square, try using one size larger needles.

Materials
2 x 50 g (2 oz) balls of chunky (bulky) Patons
  Inca, Stormy Blue
Pair of 7.5 mm knitting needles
Wool needle, for sewing up

COWL
Using 7.5 mm knitting needles and yarn, cast on 65 sts.
Row 1: *K1, P1, rep from * to last st, K1.
Rep this row until work measures 30 cm (12 in) from cast-on edge.
  Cast off loosely.
Note: It is important not to cast off tightly as it affects the drape of the garment. You can make your cowl longer, if desired, though this length provides the optimum number of soft folds.

To Make Up
With RS together, stitch the two short edges tog using mattress st. As this is a loose knit, use small stitches and be careful not to pull your work tightly or pucker the seam. Do not press.

iPad Cover

This simple envelope-style iPad cover is knitted in moss stitch. It is lined with fabric, which gives it greater strength and stability. There is very little shaping. A single ribbon tied in a bow holds the layers together.

Stitches Used
- Knit
- Purl
- Cast on
- Cast off

Materials
3 x 50 g (2 oz) balls Patons Cotton Blends DK (8 ply), Sky 10
1 x 50 g (2 oz) ball Patons Cotton Blend DK (8 ply), Cream 03
Pair of 4.5 mm (US 7) knitting needles
Wool needle, for sewing up
Polyester sewing thread
Sewing needle
0.5 m (½ yd) cotton fabric, for lining (I used Lark by Amy Butler)
1 m (1 yd) x 2 cm (¾ in) wide velvet ribbon

IPAD COVER
Using 4.5 mm (US 7) knitting needles and Sky, cast on 63 sts.
Work 4 rows garter st.
Join in Cream and work 2 rows garter st. Break off Cream.
Work another 2 rows garter st Sky.
Next row: K1, *P1, K1, rep from * to end (this forms moss st patt).

Rep this row until work measures 19 cm (7½ in).
Next row: Cast on 2 sts, cont in moss st to end of row.
Rep this row once.
Cont in moss st until work measures 48 cm (19 in).
Work 4 rows garter st in Sky.
Work 2 row garter st in Cream.
Work another 4 rows garter st in Sky.
Cast off.

To Make Up
Darn in all ends. Press piece lightly. Block into shape. Piece should measure 50 x 32 cm (20 x 13 in). Cut a piece of lining fabric 1.5 cm (½ in) larger all around than the knitted piece, then press in a 1.5 cm (½ in) hem all around. Pin to the knitted piece. When pinning ensure that the 2 extra sts cast on for each side remain unlined. Sew the lining just inside these 2 sts.

Sew the cast-on sts to each other at each side forming a tiny gusset. Fold the ribbon in half and sew in place with a few stitches to hold in place to centre back of iPad. Tie in a bow at the front.

Pull Up Your Socks

Knitting socks is one of life's great pleasures. Many socks are knitted in 4-ply yarn making them a labour of love and quite time consuming to knit. However, these knee-high boot socks are made in DK (8-ply) and because they are thicker, they are quicker to knit. I have made the cuff, heel and toe in separate solid colours to make it easy to see where you are up to if you are new to sock knitting. You can adjust the foot length to suit. There is some shaping in the calf to ensure a good fit.

Stitches Used
- Cast on
- Knit
- Slip
- Psso
- K2tog
- Purl
- Turn
- Pick up
- Grafting or Kitchener stitch (directions given at end)

Measurements
To fit: Ladies, knee high
Foot length: 25 cm (10 in) adjustable

Tension
25 sts and 34 rows to 10 cm (4 in) worked in st st on 3.25 mm (US 3) knitting needles.
Note: These socks have been worked on smaller needles than would usually be recommended for DK (8-ply), to ensure a firm elastic fit. If you have fewer stitches than the tension square specifies, try using one size smaller needles, If you have more stitches, try using a size larger needles.

Materials
2 x 50 g (2 oz) ball of DK (8-ply) Main Colour (MC)
2 x 50 g (2 oz) balls DK (8-ply) contrast (C1)
2 x 50 g (2 oz) balls DK (8-ply) contrast (C2)
Note: You will not need all this yarn. It is best to use a pure wool machine washable yarn. Acrylic is not recommended as it tends to stretch and is very harsh on the skin.
4 x 3.25 mm (US 3) double-pointed knitting needles
Wool needle, for grafting toe

SOCKS

Make 2

Using 4 x 3.25 mm (US 3) knitting needles and MC, cast on 64 sts (22, 20, 22). Join into a ring being careful not to twist sts.

Work in K1, P1 rib for 7 cm (2¾ in).

Next round: Commence stripe patt.

Stripe Pattern

Worked in stocking stitch

  2 rounds MC

  2 rounds C1

2 rounds C2

This 6-round stripe pattern is worked for the length of the calf

Continue in stripe patt until work measures 17 cm (6¾ in) from cast-on edge.

Calf Shaping

Keep continuity of stripe pattern and note that all dec rounds will fall on first round of MC.

Next round: With MC, K1, K2tog, knit to last 3 sts, Sl 1, K1, psso, K1 (62 sts).

Work another 5 rounds without shaping.

Dec round: With MC, K1, K2tog, knit to last 3 sts, Sl1, K1, psso, K1 (60 sts).

Work another 5 rounds without shaping.

Dec round: With MC, K1, K2tog, knit to last 3 sts, Sl1, K1, psso, K1 (58 sts).

Work another 5 rounds without shaping.

Dec round: With MC, K1, K2tog, knit to last 3 sts, Sl1, K1, psso, K1 (56 sts).

Cont in stripe patt without further shaping until work measures 28 cm (11 in) from cast-on edge (the length of leg can be altered at this point if you want longer or shorter socks.

Beg Heel: (Note: Heel is knitted in C2)

Knit the first 14 sts on to a needle. Next slip the last 14 sts from **the third needle** onto this same needle (28 heels sts). (You will now work backward and forward in rows on these sts to create the heel flap). Divide the remaining 28 sts on to 2 needles and leave at front of work for instep.

Row 1: Sl1, purl to end of row.

Row 2: Sl 1, *K1, Sl 1, rep from * to end of row. Rep these 2 rows 9 times then Row 1 once (21 heel rows).

To Turn the Heel (This gives you the curved shape for your heel to fit into)

Next row: K17, K2tog, K1, turn, P8, P2tog, P1, turn, K9, K2tog, K1, turn, P10, P2tog, P1, turn, K11, K2tog, K1, turn, cont in this manner, (working 1 more st each time until all sts are worked on to 1 needle (18 sts).

Next row: K9 (this completes the heel). Slip all instep stitches back on to one needle. Break off C2 and join in C1.

Next: With your empty needle and starting at the centre point of the heel, knit the remaining 9 heel sts, pick up and knit 12 sts along the side of the heel flap; With second needle, knit across 28 instep st; with third needle, pick up and knit 12 sts along other side of heel flap, knit remaining 9 heels sts (70 sts).

Your knitting is now back in the round.

Shaping the Instep

Round 1: Using C1, knit.

Round 2: First needle: Knit to last 4 sts, K2tog, K2. Second needle: knit. Third needle: K2, Sl 1, K1, psso, knit to end of round.

Rep these 2 rounds until 14 sts rem on needles 1 and 3, and 28 sts rem on needle 2.

Continue in st st without further shaping until

work measures 15 cm (6 in) from where sts were picked up from side of heel. (Note: Foot length can be lengthened or shortened here if desired.)

Shape Toe

Round 1: Change to MC and knit.

Round 2: First needle: Knit to last 4 sts, K2tog, K2. Second needle: K2, Sl 1, K1, psso, knit to last 4 sts, K2tog, K2. Third needle K2, Sl 1, K1, psso, knit to end of round.

Rep these 2 rounds until 6 sts rem on needles 1 and 3, and 12 sts rem on needle 2. With needle 3, knit the sts from needle 1 so that you have 12 sts on 2 needles facing each other ready for grafting.

To Graft Toe

Grafting is an excellent way of invisibly joining two pieces of knitting. The edges are not cast off and the knitting can be joined either while it is still on the needles, or after it has been taken off.

Grafting with Knitting on the Needles

Thread a wool or tapestry needle with a length of knitting yarn. Place the two pieces to be joined with right sides facing and hold the knitting needles in the left hand. Pass the wool needle knitwise through the first stitch on the front needle and slip the stitch off the knitting needle. Pass the wool needle purlwise through the second stitch on the same needle, leaving the stitch on the needle. Pass purlwise through the first stitch on the back knitting needle and slip the stitch off, then pass knitwise through the second stitch on the same needle, leaving the stitch on the needle. Repeat from *.

Darn in all loose ends and press lightly if needed.

Purple Patch Knitted Cushion

If you are fairly new to knitting or are not particularly confident with patterns involving a lot of shaping then cushion covers are for you. Cushion covers are straightforward to make and very useful. Use them to brighten up an old sofa, personalise your bedroom or to add comfort. This cushion is a chunky, bold affair, knitted in a pure wool bouclé, with a chunky wool on the back. Big wooden buttons really highlight its simple appeal.

Stitches Used
- Cast On
- Cast off
- Knit
- Purl

Measurements
Fits a 38 cm (15 in) cushion insert.
Back panel: 40 x 45 cm (15¾ x 17¾ in)
Front panel: 40 cm (15¾ in) square.

Tension
Passioknit Baroque 'Armytage' – 8 sts and 11 rows to 10 cm (4 in) st st on 10 mm (US 15) knitting needles
Passioknit Baroque 'Vervale' 12 sts and 16 rows to 10 cm worked over gt st on 7 mm knitting needles

Materials
5 x 50 g (2 oz) balls of Passioknit Baroque 'Armytage' (Super Chunky) Dark Purple
4 x 50 g (2 oz) balls of Passioknit Baroque 'Vervale' (Chunky Bouclé) Dark Purple
Pair of 10 mm (US 15) knitting needles
Pair of 7 mm knitting needles
4 wooden buttons, each 4 cm (1¾ in) diameter
38 cm (14 in) cushion insert
Wool needle, for sewing up
Small amount of Dark Purple DK (8-ply) yarn, for sewing up
Polyester sewing thread and sewing needle

CUSHION BACK
Using 10 mm (US 15) knitting needles and Baroque 'Armytage', cast on 30 sts.
Work 4 rows garter st
Cont in st st until work measures 41 cm (16¼ in) from cast-on edge.
Work 2 rows garter st.
Buttonhole row: K5, *cast off 2 sts, K4, rep from * to last 5 sts, K5.
Next row: K5, *turn, cast on 2 sts, turn, K4, rep from * to last 5 sts, K5.
Knit 1 row.
Cast off. Darn in all loose ends.

CUSHION FRONT

The front of the cushion is made from 16 garter
st patches, each knitted in Baroque 'Vervale'.
Using 7 mm knitting needles and yarn, cast on
12 sts. Knit 18 rows garter st.
Cast off.

To Make Up

The garter st patches are joined lengthways
in strips of 4. Then the 4 strips are stitched
together along their side seams to create the
cushion front.

Use small stitches and the DK (8-ply) yarn
to sew the pieces together. Place the complete
front panel on top of the back panel, RS tog,
matching the bottom edges. Pin in place,
matching side and bottom seams. The back is
longer than the front. This is correct. Carefully
and firmly stitch in place all around the pinned
edges. Turn right way out. Fold the back flap
over the cushion front and stitch down the sides
6 cm (2¼ in) on each side. Mark the positions
for the buttons with a pin approximately 5 cm
(2 in) down from the top edge and stitch the
buttons in place with matching sewing thread.
Insert the cushion pad into the cushion cover
and close the button. Check for any loose ends
or leftover pins.

Purple Power

This very simple slouchie hat is an excellent project for the beginner knitter as it uses only stocking stitch and very simple increases to create a great wearable and stylish hat for the winter months.

~~~~~~

Stitches Used

- Cast on
- Cast off
- Inc 1
- Knit
- K2tog
- M1
- Purl
- Stocking stitch

Tension

20 sts and 28 rows to 10 cm (4 in) square worked over st st.

Note: If you have fewer sts than specified, try knitting the tension square with one size smaller needles. If you have more stitches than specified across the tension square, try using one size larger needles.

Materials

1 x 100 g (3½ oz) ball of DK (8-ply) Cleckheaton California Purple

Pair of 4.5 mm (US 7) knitting needles

Wool needle, for sewing up

HAT

Using 4.5 mm (US 7) knitting needles and DK (8-ply) yarn, cast on 100 sts.

Row 1: Purl.

Row 2: Purl.

Cont in st st until work measures 13.5 cm (5½ in) from beg.

Increase row: *K10, m1, rep from * to last st inc in last st.

Work 3 rows st st.

Next row: *K11, m1, rep from * to last st inc in last st.

Work 3 rows st st.

Next row: *K12, m1, rep from * to last st inc in last st.

Work another 7 rows st st.

Begin Decreases for Crown

Next row: *K11, K2tog, rep from * rep from * to end.

Work 3 rows st st.

Next row: *K10, K2tog, rep from * rep from * to end.

Work 3 rows st st.

Next row: *K9, K2tog, rep from * rep from * to end.

Purl 1 row.

Next row: *K1, K2tog, rep from * to last st, K1.

Purl 1 row.
Next row: *K2tog, rep from * to end.
Purl 1 row.
Repeat last 2 rows once.
Break off yarn, thread through rem sts, pull up tightly and fasten off.

To Make Up
Depending upon yarn used, press knitting fabric lightly, using a warm iron and a damp cloth. With RS tog, stitch back seam using a fine back stitch. Darn in any loose ends.

Note: As you become a more experienced knitter you could easily knit this hat on a circular needle or a set of four double-pointed knitting needles and this would do away with the back seam.

Remembrance Day Brooch

This knitted poppy and leaf brooch is easy to make and will look stylish pinned to a winter coat or hat. It is mainly knitted in garter stitch and uses DK (8-ply) wool.

~~~~~~

Stitches Used

- Cast on
- Cast off
- Garter stitch
- K2tog
- Sl 1, K1 psso
- Sl 2, K1 psso
- Yfwd

Materials

Less than 50 g (2 oz) DK (8-ply) pure wool, Red
Less than 50 g (2 oz) DK (8-ply) pure wool, Black
Tiny amount of DK (8-ply), Green, for flower centre
2 mm (US 0) double-pointed knitting needles
3 mm (US 2½) double-pointed knitting needles
Wool needle
1.5 cm (¾ in) metal brooch back
1.5 cm (¾ in) square of black felt
Polyester thread and sewing needle

Measurements

10 cm (4 in) long

Note: The tension is tighter than would be usual for DK (8-ply), as this project is knitted on 3 mm (US 2½) knitting needles

POPPY PETALS

Make 4
Using 3 mm (US 2½) double-pointed knitting needles and Red, cast on 7 sts.
Row 1: Knit.
Row 2: Inc in first st, knit to last 2 sts, inc in next st, K1 (9 sts).
Row 3: As for Row 2 (11 sts).
Row 4: As for Row 2 (13 sts).
Rows 5–8: Knit.
Row 9: Sl 1, K1, psso, twice, knit to last 4 sts, K2tog twice (9 sts).
Rows 10–12: Knit.
Row 13: As Row 9 (5 sts).
Rows 14–16: Knit.
Row 17: K1, Sl 2, K1, psso, K1 (3 sts).
Row 18: Knit.
Cast off.

CENTRE OF POPPY

Using 3 mm (US 2½) double-pointed knitting needles and Green, cast on 16 sts. Cast off.

To Make Up

Join the cast-off edges of the petals together in pairs and then place one pair over the other to form a cross-like formation and secure with a few stiches. Coil the green centre piece up very tightly and stitch in place. Using black yarn, work French knots around the green centre. To maintain the cupped shape of the poppy, place a small stitch behind each pair of petals.

I-CORD LEAVES
Make 2

Using 3 mm (US 2½) double-pointed knitting needles and Black, cast on 3 sts. Knit 1 row. Without turning, slide the stiches to the opposite end of the needle. Take the yarn firmly across the wrong side of the work from left to right and knit 1 row. Repeat from *, or until the I-cord is 1.5 cm (¾ in) long.

Row 1 (RS): K1, yfwd, K1, yfwd, K1 (5 sts).
Row 2: K2, P1, K2.
Row 3: K2, yfwd, K1, yfwd, K2 (7 sts).
Rows 4, 6, 8, 10, 12 and 14: Knit all sts except for centre st, which is purled.
Row 5: K3, yfwd, K1, yfwd, K3 (9 sts).
Row 7: K4, yfwd, K1, yfwd, K4 (11 sts).
Row 9: K5, yfwd, K1, yfwd, K5 (13 sts).
Row 11: K6, yfwd, K1, yfwd, K6 (15 sts).
Row 13: K7, yfwd, K1, yfwd, K7 (17 sts).
Row 16 and all even rows: Knit.
Row 17: Sl 1, K1, psso, K13, K2tog (15 sts).
Row 19: Sl 1, K1, psso, K11, K2tog (13 sts).
Row 21: Sl 1, K1, psso, K9, K2tog (11 sts).
Row 23: Sl 1, K1, psso, K7, K2tog (9 sts).
Row 25: Sl 1, K1, psso, K5 K2tog (7 sts).
Row 27: Sl 1, K1, psso, K3, K2tog (5 sts).
Row 29: Sl 1, K1, psso, K1, K2tog (3 sts).
Row 31: Sl 2, K1, psso, Fasten off rem st.
Darn in all loose ends

To Make Up

Cut a small piece of black felt slightly larger than the metal bar on the base of the brooch. Arrange the 2 leaves with the tips pointing down and the flower in front. Stitch all to the piece of felt using very small stitches. Sew the whole flower to the brooch base securing it through the holes in that item. Stitch from the outside edge and into the centre of each hole from each side. This way your pieces are securely held in place.

Time for Tea Knitted Tea Cosy

Once you have mastered the basics of knitting you may like to make a tea cosy? This one looks fantastic, and has very little shaping. It is not lined, but its voluminous shape will trap the warm air between the pot and the cosy keeping your tea hot, (especially if you knit with pure wool).

Stitches Used

- Cast on
- Cast off
- Knit
- Purl
- Yfwd
- K2tog

Measurement

To fit a 6-cup teapot
20 x 62 cm diameter (8 x 24½ in)

Tension

22.5 sts and 30 rows to 10 cm (4 in) of st st worked on 4 mm (US 6) knitting needles.
Note: If you have fewer sts than specified, try knitting the tension square with one size smaller needles. If you have more stitches than specified across the tension square, try using one size larger needles.

Materials

1 x 50 g (2 oz) ball DK (8-ply) pure wool, in choice of colour
45 cm (17¾ in) of 1.5 cm (¾ in) wide ribbon
18 felt hearts
Pair of 4 mm (US 6) knitting needles
Wool needle, for sewing up

Sewing needle and sewing cotton, for attaching felt hearts

TEA COSY

Make 2
Using 4 mm (US 6) knitting needles and DK (8-ply) yarn, cast on 58 sts.
Work 6 rows garter st.
Next row: Knit.
Next row: K4, purl to last 4 sts, K4.
Rep these last 2 rows until work measures 17 cm (6¾ in) from cast-on edge, ending with a purl row.

Shape Top

Next row: K4, K2tog, *K2, K2tog, rep from * to last 4 sts, K4.
Next row: K4, purl to last 4 sts, K4.
Next row: K4, *yfwd, K2tog, rep from * to last 4 sts, K4.
Work another 12 rows garter st.
Cast off.

To Make Up

Press pieces lightly using a damp cloth and a warm iron. Arrange 9 felt hearts on the right side of each piece. Once you are happy with the arrangement, carefully stitch the hearts to the tea cosy using the sewing needle and matching

thread, and taking very small stitches right through both pieces. If your stitches are very small and tight they will disappear in the felt and will not be seen.

With RS tog, stitch the lower 2 cm (¾ in) and top 2 cm (¾ in) on each side. This leaves an opening for the handle and the spout. Darn in any loose ends. Turn the right way out. Find the centre eyelet hole on one side and begin threading the ribbon through the eyelet holes at this point. Cont all the way around until it comes out just opposite where it went in. Pull up tightly and tie into a firm bow.

Ruby Scarf

This simple chunky ribbed scarf is made using just two stitches: knit and purl. By using a great yarn in a fantastic shade you can knit up a beautiful scarf in next to no time.

Stitches Used

- Knit
- Purl
- Cast on
- Cast off

Materials

8 balls Moda Vera Manor (chunky)
Pair of 6.5 mm (US 10½) knitting needles
Wool needle, for sewing in ends

Tension

20 sts and 15 rows worked over rib pattern on 6.5 mm (US 10½) knitting needles (not stretched)

SCARF

Using 6.5 mm (US 10½) knitting needles and yarn, cast on 45 sts.

Row 1: *K3, P3, rep from * to end.

Row 2: *P3, K3, rep from * to end.

Repeat these 2 rows until work measures 1.5 m (60 in).

Cast off in rib. Darn in all ends.

Note: When joining in a new ball of yarn, do this at the end of a row for a neater finish and to make darning the ends in much easier.

Ruby Slippers

If you can knit, purl and cast on and off you can make these slippers. They are very soft and warm, ideal for wearing when curling up on the sofa with a good book. A little crocheted edging makes them very feminine. The alternate pair features a row of eyelets holes through which you can thread a lovely velvet ribbon. These knit up quickly and would make a great Mother's Day or Christmas gift.

Stitches Used
- Knit
- Purl
- Yfwd
- K2tog
- Sl 1, K1, psso
- Cast on
- Cast off

Crochet
- Chain
- Sl st
- dc

Measurements
Approximately 10 cm (4 in) deep x 23/25.5/28 cm (9/10/11 in) long (small, medium, large)

Materials
2 x 50 g (2 oz) balls of Patons Inca (Chunky) shade 7040, Crimson
Pair of 5.5 mm (US 9) knitting needles
Wool needle, for sewing up
2 stitch markers
For ribbon slippers: 1 m (yd) x 1.5 cm (¾ in) wide velvet ribbon
Small amounts of DK (8-ply) in 2 different shades, for flowers
Small amounts of DK (8-ply) in two shades of green, for leaves
2 mm (US 0) double-pointed knitting needles
3 mm (US 2½) double-pointed knitting needles
4 mm (US G/6) crochet hook
Polyester thread and sewing needle

SLIPPERS
Make 2
Using 5.5 mm (US 9) knitting needles and yarn, cast on 41 (46, 55) sts.

Row 1: Knit

Rows 2 and 3: Knit.

Row 4: K20 (23, 27), place markers, K1, knit to end of row.

Row 5: K20 (23, 27), yfwd, K1, yfwd, knit to end of row.

Row 6 and all even rows: Purl.

Row 7: K20 (23, 27), yfwd, K3, yfwd, knit to end of row.

Row 9: K20 (23, 27), yfwd, K5, yfwd, knit to end of row.

Row 11: K20 (23, 27), yfwd, K7, yfwd, knit to end of row.

Row 13: K20 (23, 27), yfwd, K9, yfwd, knit to end of row.

Purl 1 row.

Work another 8 rows st st, beg with a knit row. Cast off.

To Make Up

With RS tog and using back stitch, sew the heel and sole seams. Keep sts close tog, aiming for a neat finish. Turn the slipper the right way out. Do not press.

FLOWERS

Make 3 for the toe of the slipper using different shades for the inner and outer petals

Centre: Using shade A, make a slip ring.

Round 1 RS: 3ch, 15 tr into ring, pull the end to close the ring, sl st, into top of third ch (16 sts).

Round 2: 4ch, (Ss in the front strand of next tr, 3ch) 15 times, sl st into first of 4ch. Fasten off neatly.

Second round of petals (RS): Working behind Round 2 and into the Round 1, join in a contrast colour in the top ch of 3ch, 6ch, working in the back strand of each tr; (sl st in next tr, 5ch) 15 times, sl st in first of 6ch. Fasten off neatly. Make another flower altering the colours.

LEAVES

Using 2.25 mm (US 1) knitting needles and 4-ply Bright Green, cast on 3 sts. Work an I-cord for 1.5 cm (¾ in).

Row 1 RS: Knit.

Row 2 and all even rows: Knit.

Row 3: K1, m1, K1, m1, K1.

Row 5: K2, m1, K1, m1, K2.

Row 7: K3, m1, K1, m1, K3.

Row 9: K4, m1, K1, m1, K4.

Row 11: K5, m1, K1, m1, K5.

Rows 13 and 15: Knit.

Row 17: K5, Sl 2, K1, psso, K5.

Row 19: K4, Sl 2, K1, psso, K4.

Row 21: K3, Sl 2, K1, psso, K3.

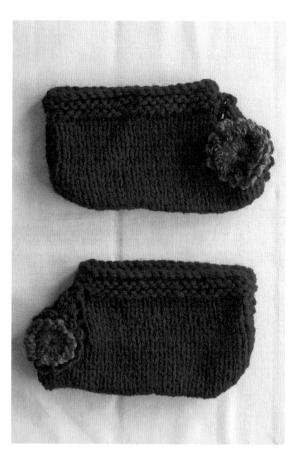

Row 23: K2, Sl 2, K1, psso, K2.

Row 25: K1, Sl 2, K1, psso, K1 (3 sts).

Row 27: K1, Sl 2, psso, fasten off.

To Make Up

Darn in all ends on the leaves and flowers and then arrange them on the toe of the slippers. It may be easier to try the slipper on your foot to do this as the shape will be defined. Pin the flowers and leaves in position and then stitch in place using matching thread.

SLIPPERS WITH RIBBON

Make 2

Using 5.5 mm (US 9) knitting needles and Patons Inca, cast on 41 (46, 55) sts.

Row 1: Knit

Row 2: K1, *yfwd, K2tog, rep from* to end, (last st, K1).

Row 3: Knit.

Row 4: K20, (23, 27) place markers, K1, Knit to end of row.

Row 5: K20, (23, 27), yfwd, K1, yfwd, knit to end of row.

Row 6 and all even rows: Purl.

Row 7: K20 (23, 27), yfwd, K3, yfwd, knit to end of row.

Row 9: K20 (23, 27), yfwd, K5, yfwd, knit to end of row.

Row 11: K20 (23, 27), yfwd, K7, yfwd, knit to end of row.
Row 13: K20 (23, 27), yfwd, K9, yfwd, knit to end of row.
Purl 1 row.
Work another 8 rows st st, beg with a knit row.
Cast off.

To Make Up
With RS tog and using back stitch, sew the heel and sole seams. Keep sts close tog, aiming for a neat finish. Turn the slipper the right way out. Do not press.

Cut a 50 cm (20 in) length of 1.5 cm (¾ in) wide ribbon and thread it through the eyelet holes, beg and ending at the centre toe section. Repeat on the other slipper. If desired, decorate the slippers with flowers and leaves.

Handy Hands Fingerless Gloves

Once you've knitted a few projects you might like to try knitting 'in the round'. This method does away with sewing up seams at the end and creates a smooth finish. These fingerless gloves feature very simple thumb shaping and are a great way to start. Noro Silk Garden is a lovely shaded yarn, which creates a random colour pattern. A buttoned tab gives them a driving glove style finish.

~~~~~~

Stitches Used

- Knit
- Purl
- Cast on
- Cast off
- Rib: K1, P1
- M1: Make 1 stitch

Measurements

22 cm (8½ in) long

Tension

20 sts and 26 rows to 10 cm (4 in) measured over st st on 3.75 mm (US 5) knitting needles

Materials

2 x 50 g (2 oz) balls of Noro Silk Garden (aran-weight), shade 326
4 x 3.75 mm (US 5) double-pointed knitting needles
2 x 1.5 cm (¾ in) diameter pale pink buttons
Wool needle, for sewing up
Sewing needle and thread
Two knitting markers

FINGERLESS GLOVES

Make 2

Using 4 x 3.75 mm (US 5) knitting needles, and yarn, cast on 43 sts (14, 14, 15). Join into a ring, being careful not to twist sts.

Work 10 rows K1, P1, rib.

Next round: Purl, dec 1 st on third needle (42 sts).

Work another 23 rows st st (every row knit).

Next round: Place markers for thumb gusset. K6, place marker, K2, place marker, knit to end of round.

Next round (inc): K6, m1, K2, m1, knit to end of round (44 sts).

Next round (inc): K6, m1, K4, m1, knit to end of round (46 sts).

Next round (inc): K6, m1, K6, m1, knit to end of round (48 sts).

Next round (inc): K6, m1, K8, m1, knit to end of round (50 sts).

Next round (inc): K6, m1, K10, m1, knit to end of round (52 sts).

Next round (inc): K6, m1, K12, m1, knit to end of round (54 sts).

Knit 1 more round without shaping.

Next round: K6, cast off 14 sts, knit to end of

round (40 sts).

Next round: Knit to cast off sts. Cast on 2 sts (it is easier to do this by turning the work around, once you have cast on 2 sts, turn your work back around) knit to the end of the round (42 sts).

Work another 7 rounds st st (every round knit).

Next round: Purl.

Work 5 rounds in K1, P1 rib.

Cast off.

STRAPS

Make 2

Using 2 x 3.75 mm (US 5) double-pointed knitting needles and yarn, cast on 6 sts.

Row 1: Knit.

Row 2: K1, P4, K1

Rep the last 2 rows 9 times

Buttonhole row: K2, cast off 2 sts, K1.

Next row: K1, P1, cast on 2 sts, P1, K1.

Next row: Knit.

Next row: K1, P4, K1.

Cast off.

To Make Up

Press pieces lightly using a warm iron and a damp cloth. Attach the strap to the side of the glove opposite to the thumb gusset and 6 cm (2¼ in) up from cast-on edge. Use the sewing thread and needle to sew the button in place under the buttonhole.

Note. This strap is for decorative purposes only. Repeat for the other glove, making sure that you have a mirror image.

Knitted Pin Cushion

This little knitted pin cushion is made by rolling up layers of garter stitch panels, a bit like making a Swiss Roll. You can push your scissors down the centre and stick the pins in anywhere. A few knitted leaves adorn the sides.

~~~~~~

Stitches Used

- Cast On
- Cast Off
- Knit
- Sl 1
- Psso
- K2tog

Measurements

27 cm (10½ in) circumference and 9 cm (3½ in) tall

Tension

24 sts and 36 rows to 10 cm (4 in) measured over garter st on 3.75 mm (US 5) knitting needles. Measure tension carefully. Note: If you have fewer sts than specified, try knitting the tension square with one size smaller needles. If you have more stitches than specified across the tension square, try using one size larger needles.

Materials

5 x 50 g (2 oz) balls of DK (8-ply) yarn in 5 shades of green (only partial balls will be needed) Shade A (Dark Green), B (Dark Sage), C (Sage), D (Lime), E (Bright Green)
Pair of 3.75 mm (US 5) knitting needles
Pair of 3.25 mm (US 3) double-pointed knitting needles
Wool needle, for sewing up

PIN CUSHION

Using 3.75 mm (US 5) knitting needles and A, cast on 22 sts. Work 38 rows garter st. Cast off. Beg at one short end, roll the piece up firmly into a tube and stitch closed along the other short end. Set aside.

Second Layer

Using 3.75 mm (US 5) knitting needles and shade B, cast on 22 sts, work 50 rows. Cast off. Take the first piece and roll the second layer around the tube, enclosing it completely. Stitch closed along the short end. Set aside.

Third Layer

Using 3.75 mm (US 5) knitting needles and shade C, cast on 22 sts, work 60 rows. Make up as for the second layer.

Fourth Layer

Using 3.75 mm (US 5) knitting needles and shade D, cast on 22 sts, work 100 rows. Make up as for the second layer.

Fifth Layer

Using 3.75 mm (US 5) knitting needles and shade E, cast on 22 sts, work 140 rows. Make up as for the second layer.

I-cord for Base

Using 2 x 3.25 mm double -pointed knitting needles and shade B, cast on 4 sts. Knit the stitches, slide them to the other end of the needle, pull the yarn firmly behind and knit the stitches again, continuing in this manner until the cord is 27 cm (10½ in) long. K2tog twice. Psso, Fasten off.

To Make Up

Pin the I-cord to the base of the pin cushion and stitch in place through the outer layer of garter st. Darn in any loose ends.

LEAVES

Make 4, 2 in Light Sage and 2 in Dark Sage

Using 3.25 mm double-pointed knitting needles and yarn, cast on 3 sts, Work an I-cord as above until it is 1.5 cm (¾ in) long.

Row 1 (RS): K1, yfwd, K1, yfwd, K1 (5 sts).

Row 2: K2, P1, K2.

Row 3: K2, yfwd, K1, yfwd, K2 (7 sts).

Rows 4, 6, 8, 10, 12 and 14: Knit all sts except for centre st, which is purled.

Row 5: K3, yfwd, K1, yfwd, K3 (9 sts).

Row 7: K4, yfwd, K1, yfwd, K4 (11 sts).

Row 9: K5, yfwd, K1, yfwd, K5 (13 sts).

Row 11: K6, yfwd, K1, yfwd, K6 (15 sts)

Row 13: K7, yfwd, K1, yfwd, K7 (17 sts).

Row 14 and all even rows: Knit.

Row 15: Sl 1, K1, psso, K13, K2tog (15 sts).

Row 17: Sl 1, K1, psso, K11, K2tog (13 sts).

Row 19: Sl 1, K1, psso, K9, K2tog (11 sts).

Row 21: Sl 1, K1, psso, K7, K2tog (9 sts).

Row 22: Sl 1, K1, psso, K5 K2tog (7 sts).

Row 23: Sl 1, K1, psso, K3, K2tog (5 sts).

Row 27: Sl 1, K1, psso, K1, K2tog (3 sts).

Row 28: Sl 2, K1, psso. Fasten off rem st.

Darn in all loose ends

To Make Up

Pin the leaves evenly around the pin cushion and stitch the stem and the point of the leaves into place with the tips of the leaves facing downward. Darn in any loose ends.

Super Soft Slipper Socks

There comes a time in every knitter's life when they want to make socks. Socks are great. They involve no sewing up and they can easily be tailored to fit different sized feet. This is a great beginners sock project as these socks are knitted in DK (8-ply) and have relatively little shaping. Take your time while knitting and remember that with the exception of the heel you will be knitting in rounds. These slipper socks have a rolled cuff, and a ribbed panel around the ankle to hold them snuggly in place.

Stitches Used

- Knit
- Purl
- Slip 1
- Psso
- K2tog
- Grafting or Kitchener stitch

Materials

2 x 50 g (2 oz) balls DK (8-ply) pure wool, main colour
1 x 50 g (2 oz) ball DK (8-ply) pure wool, contrast
4 x 3.75 mm (US 5) double-pointed knitting needles
Wool needle, for grafting toe

Measurements

To fit: Ladies medium shoe size (5–8)

Tension

26 sts and 26 rows to 10 cm (4 in) measured over st st on 3.75 mm (US 5) knitting needles.
Note: This tension is tighter than would normally be used for 8 ply (DK).

SLIPPER SOCKS

Make 2
Using 4 x 3.75 mm (US 5) double-pointed knitting needles, and contrast yarn, cast on 42 sts (22, 10, 10).

Cuff
Work 10 rounds st st.
Work another 5 rounds K1, P1 rib. Break off contrast colour and join in main colour.

Heel
Work the heel backward and forward in rows on the first 22 sts in main colour.
With RS facing:
Row 1: Sl 1, *K1, Sl 1, K1 rep from * to end of row.
Row 2: S1, purl to end of row.
Rep these 2 rows another 12 times (26 rows) in total.

To Turn Heel
With RS facing:
Row 1: Sl 1, K12, Sl 1, K1, psso, K1, turn.
Row 2: Sl 1, P5, P2tog, P1, turn
Row 3: Sl 1, K6, Sl 1, K1, psso, K1, turn.
Row 4: Sl 1, P7, P2tog, P1, turn.
Row 5: Sl 1, K8, Sl 1, K1, psso, K1, turn.

Row 6: Sl 1, P9, P2tog, P1, turn.

Row 7: Sl 1, K10, Sl 1, K1, psso, K1, turn.

Row 8: Sl 1, P11, P2tog, P1, turn.

14 heel sts now remain.

Slip all the instep sts (these are the sts held on the remaining two needles) on to one needle. With RS of the work facing you, knit the first 7 of the heels sts. Take a new needle and knit the next 7 heel sts. With this same needle, pick up and K14 along the edge of the heel flap. With another needle knit across the 20 instep sts. With a new needle pick up and K14 stitches along the other side of heel flap. With this same needle, knit the remaining 7 heel sts (62 sts in total) 42 sole stitches and 20 instep stitches.

Shaping the Instep

Round 1: Knit.

Round 2: First needle, knit to last 4 stitches K2tog, K2. Second needle, knit. Third needle, K2, Sl 1, K1, psso, knit remaining sts.

Repeat these two rounds until 11 sts remain on needles 1 and 3, and 20 sts remain on needle 2 (42 sts).

Cont knitting without further shaping until foot measures 15 cm (6 in) from where stiches were picked up at side of heel (This will give a size 6/7 slipper). You can increase the length of your slipper at this point, if you like.

Shape Toe

Break off Main Colour and join in Contrast.

Knit 1 round.

Round 1: Knit.

Round 2: First needle, knit to last 4 sts, K2tog, K2. Second needle, knit. Third needle, K2, Sl 1, K1, psso, knit to end.

Round 3: First needle, knit to last 4 sts, K2tog, K2. Second needle, K2, Sl 1, K1, psso, knit to

last 4 sts, K2tog, K2. Third needle, K2, Sl 1, K1, psso, knit to end.

Repeat rounds 1 and 3 until 5 sts remain on needles 1 and 3, and 10 sts remain on needle 2.

To Graft Toe

Grafting is an excellent way of invisibly joining two pieces of knitting. The edges are not cast off and the knitting can be joined either while it is still on the needles, or after it has been taken off.

Grafting with Knitting on the Needles

Thread a wool or tapestry needle with a length of knitting yarn. Place the two pieces to be joined with right sides facing and hold the knitting needles in the left hand. Pass the wool needle knitwise through the first stitch on the front needle and slip the stitch off the knitting needle. Pass the wool needle purlwise through the second stitch on the same needle, leaving the stitch on the needle. Pass purlwise through the first stitch on the back knitting needle and slip the stitch off, then pass knitwise through the second stitch on the same needle, leaving the stitch on the needle. Repeat.

Darn in all loose ends and press lightly if needed.

Striped Hottie Cover

A practical knitted project to help warm cold toes in winter. This hot water bottle cover uses simple stiches and no shaping to great effect. Slip a filled hot water bottle in the drawstring opening at the top and put your feet up.

~~~~~~

Stitches Used

- Knit
- Purl
- K2tog
- P2tog
- Yrn
- Cast on
- Cast off

Materials

2 x 50 g (2 oz) balls DK (8-ply) pure wool, Red
1 x 50 g (2 oz) ball balls DK (8-ply) pure wool, Cream
Pair of 4 mm (US 6) knitting needles
Wool needle, for sewing up
90 cm (35 in) x 1.5 cm (¾ in) wide red velvet ribbon

Measurements

19.5 x 27.5 cm (7½ x 11 in)

Tension

22 sts and 28 rows to 10 cm (4 in) worked in st st on 4 mm (US 6) knitting needles over striped pattern.

HOT WATER BOTTLE COVER

Make 2
Using 4 mm (US 6) knitting needles and Red, cast on 58 sts.
Row 1: *K2, P2, rep from * to end of row.
Row 2: *P2, K2, rep from * to end of row.
Repeat these 2 rows another 7 times (16 rows rib in all).
Eyelet row: *K2, yrn, P2tog, rep from * to end.
Repeat Row 2 and then Row 1 once more.
Next row: K2tog, knit to last 2 sts, K2tog (56 sts).
Next row: Purl.
Join in Cream and work 2 rows st st.
Cont in stripes of 2 rows Red, 2 rows Cream until there are 19 Cream stripes.
Cast off on the next knit row in Red.

To Make Up

Press the pieces lightly using a damp cloth and a warm iron. With RS tog and using back stitch, join pieces tog leaving top open. Turn RS out. Thread the ribbon through the eyelet holes beginning and ending at the centre front. Tie into a bow and trim off any excess length. If you cut your ribbon ends on the diagonal it will stop them from fraying.

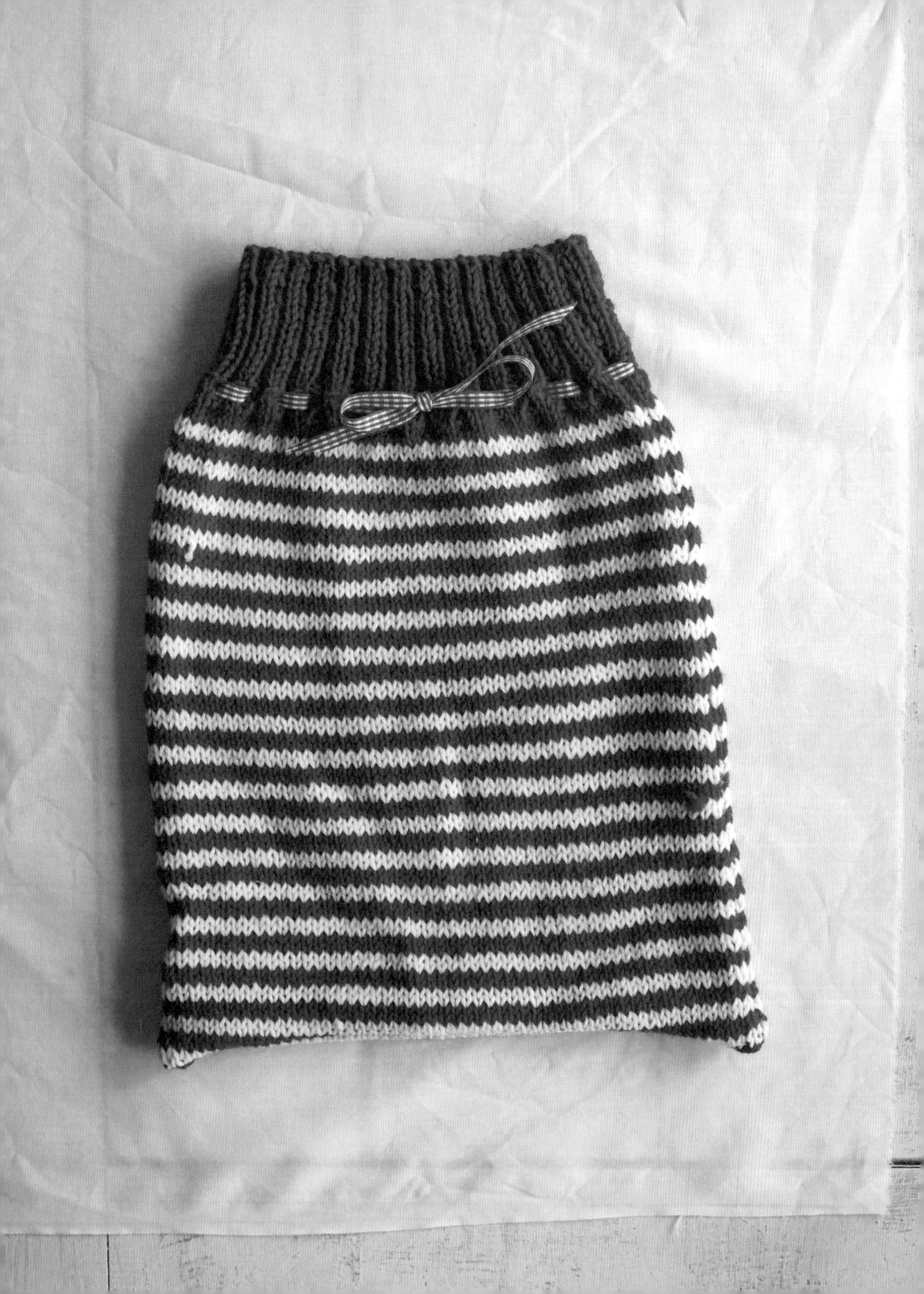

The Knitter's Bag

This knitted bag is the perfect size to hold your knitting while out and about. It is fabric-lined so it won't stretch out of shape and it is just the right size for storing your current project and pattern. A simple knit and purl stitch pattern provides an interesting textural fabric. Choose your favourite colour in DK (8-ply) and a complementary lining fabric.

Stitches Used
- Cast on
- Cast off
- Knit
- Purl
- Yfwd
- K2tog
- Garter stitch: Every row knit

Measurements
37 x 38 cm (14½ x 15 in), not including handles

Tension
20 sts and 24 rows to 10 cm (4 in) of circles stitch pattern worked on 4.5 mm (US 7) knitting needles

Materials
5 x 50 g (2 oz) balls of pure wool DK (8-ply), Purple
Pair of 4.5 mm (US 7) knitting needles
Wool needle, for sewing up
90 cm (35 in) x 1 cm (3/8 in) wide velvet ribbon
1 m (40 in) cotton fabric, for lining
Polyester sewing thread and needle
Sewing machine

CIRCLE STITCH PATTERN
Note: This is a 20-row pattern repeat.
Row 1: (WS) Purl.
Row 2: Knit.
Row 2: P4, *K3, P7, rep from * to last 7 sts, K3, P4.
Row 4: K3, *P5, K5, rep from * to last 8 sts, P5, K3.
Rows 5 and 7: P2, *K7, P3, rep from * to last 9 sts, K7, P2
Rows 6 and 8: K2, *P7, K3, rep from * to last 9 sts, P7, K2.
Row 9: P3, *K5, P5, rep from * to last 8 sts, K5, P3.
Row 10: K4, *P3, K7 rep from * to last 7 sts, P3, K4.
Row 11: Purl.
Row 12: Knit.
Row 13: K2, *P7, K3, rep from * to last 9 sts, P7, K2.
Row 14: P3, *K5, P5, rep from * to last 8 sts, K5, P3.
Rows 15 and 17: K4, *P3, K7 rep from * to last 7 sts, P3, K4.
Rows 16 and 18: P4, *K3, P7, rep from * to last 7 sts, K3, P4.
Row 19: K3, *P5, K5, rep from * to last 8 sts, P5,

K3.

Row 20: P2, *K7, P3, rep from * to last 9 sts, K7, P2.

BAG

Make 2

Using 4.5 mm (US 7) knitting needles and yarn, cast on 71 sts.

Work 10 rows garter st (every row knit).

Work 4 complete 20-row pattern repeats (80 rows in total).

Next row: Purl.

Eyelet row: *K1, yfwd, K2tog, rep from * to last 2 sts, K2, ywfd, K2tog. Beg with a purl row, work 8 rows st st.

Picot row: K1, *yfwd, K2tog, rep from * to end. Work another 7 rows st st, beg with a purl row. Cast off.

HANDLES

Make 2

Using 4.5 mm (US 7) knitting needles and yarn, cast on 70 sts.

Work 2 rows garter st.

Beg with a knit row, work 7 rows st st.

Work 2 rows garter st.

Cast off purlwise.

To Make Up

Press pieces carefully and block into shape using a damp cloth and a warm iron. Darn in all loose ends. Place the main pieces of the bag together with RS facing and stitch the side and bottom seams closed using a back stitch. Turn the top hem over at the picot row and stitch to the inside edge.

Cut a piece of lining 39 x 71 cm (15¼ x 28 in). Fold in half, RS tog and then measure it against the bag so that when the hem is folded at the top it comes to just below the first row of eyelet holes. Press this hem in place to the inside. Stitch the side seams of the lining. Slip the lining inside the knitted bag with WS facing. Using polyester thread and a sewing needle, slip stitch the lining in place just below the row of eyelets. Use very small stitches and make them close together so the lining is firmly attached.

Thread the ribbon through the eyelet holes beg and ending at the middle of one side. Tie into a bow and neaten the ends, if needed.

Lining Handles

Cut 2 pieces of lining fabric 43 x 8 cm (17 x 3½ in). Place the knitted piece over the top, WS tog and fold in the hems. Press the hems flat using a warm iron. Pin in place all around and then stitch the fabric lining to the knitted piece. Use a blind hem stitch and small stitches. Remember handles receive plenty of wear so take your time and make your stitches small.

Sew 1 handle to each side of the bag, approximately 6 cm (2½ in) in for the side edge and at the lower edge of the picot hem. Use wool to attach the handles and ensure that your stitches are small and firmly attached.

Warm in Winter

Gloves are a project for someone with a little knitting experience and I would wait until you have knitted a few other designs and gained a little confidence before thinking about starting this project. These fingerless gloves are knitted on two needles in DK (8-ply) and require a bit of patience while sewing up in order to achieve a really good result. Be sure to use pure wool so that they are warm and soft to wear.

Stitches Used
- Cast on
- Cast off
- Knit
- Purl
- K2tog
- M1 by picking up the loop between the stich just knitted and the next one on the needle, and knitting into the back of it.

Materials
2 x 50 g (2 oz) balls of DK (8-ply) pure wool, Red
Pair of 3 mm (US 2½) knitting needles
Pair of 3.75 mm (US 5) knitting needles
Wool needle, for sewing up

Measurements
To fit ladies hand, approximately 18.5 cm (7¼ in) long

Tension
23.5 sts to 10 cm (4 in) over st st.
Note: Tension is tighter than would usually be advised for DK (8-ply) as smaller needles are being used to produce a firmer knitted fabric. Check tension carefully.

RIGHT FINGERLESS GLOVE

Using 3 mm (US 2½) knitting needles and yarn, cast on 42 sts.
Work 20 rows K1, P1 rib.
Change to 3.75 mm (US 5) knitting needles.
Row 1: Knit.
Row 2: K1, purl to last st, K1.**
Row 3: K22, m1, K1, m1, K19.
Rows 4, 5 and 6: St st.
Row 7: K22, m1, K3, m1, K19.
Rows 8, 9 and 10: St st.
Row 11: K22, m1, K5, m1, K19.
Cont in this manner, inc 2 sts on every fourth row until there are 52 sts.
Work 1 row.

Thumb
Next row: K34, turn.
Next row: K1, P12, turn, cast on 3 sts.
Work 4 rows st st on these 16 sts, followed by 2 rows of K1, P1 rib.
Cast off in rib.
With RS facing, join in yarn and knit 3 sts from cast-on sts at base of thumb, knit to end (42 sts).
Work 11 rows st st.

First Finger

Next row: K27, turn.

Next row: K1, P11, turn, cast on 2 sts.

Work 4 rows st st on these 15 sts, followed by 2 rows of K1, P1 rib.

Cast off in rib.

Second Finger

With RS facing, join in yarn and K2 sts from cast-on sts at base of first finger, K5, turn.

Next row: K1, P11, turn, cast on 2 sts.

Work 4 rows st st on these 14 sts, followed by 2 rows of K1, P1 rib.

Cast off in rib.

Third Finger

With RS facing, join in yarn and K2 sts from cast-on sts at base of second finger, K5, turn.

Next row: K1, P11, turn, cast on 2 sts.

Work 4 rows st st on these 14 sts, followed by 2 rows of K1, P1 rib.

Cast off in rib.

Fourth Finger

With RS facing, join in yarn and knit up 2 sts from cast-on sts at base of third finger, K5.

Next row: K1, P10, K1.

Work 4 rows st st on these 12 sts, followed by two rows of K1, P1 rib.

Cast off in rib.

LEFT FINGERLESS GLOVE

Work as for Right Fingerless Glove to **

Row 3: K19, m1, K1, m1, K22.

Rows 4, 5 and 6: St st.

Row 7: K19, m1, K3, m1, K22.

Rows 8, 9 and 10: St st.

Row 11: K19, m1, K5, m1, K22.

Cont in this manner, increasing 2 sts in every fourth row until there are 52 sts.

Work 1 row.

Thumb

Next row: K31, turn and cast on 3 sts.

Next row: K1, P14, K1, turn.

Complete as for Right Glove.

With RS facing, join in yarn and K3 sts from cast-on sts at base of thumb, knit to end (42 sts).

Work 11 rows st st.

First Finger

Next row: K27, turn and cast on 2 sts.

Next row: K1, P12, K1, turn.

Complete as for Right Glove.

Second Finger

With RS facing, join in yarn and K2 sts from cast-on sts at base of first finger, K5, turn and cast on 2 sts.

Next row: K1, P12, K1, turn.

Complete as for Right Glove.

Third Finger

With RS facing, join in yarn and K2 sts from cast-on sts at base of second finger, K5, turn and cast on 2 sts.

Next row: K1, P12, K1, turn.

Complete as for Right Glove.

Fourth Finger

Work as for Right Glove.

To Make Up

Press lightly using a damp cloth and a warm iron. This really does making sewing seams much easier and neater and is a great help with gloves because you want your seams to be fine and therefore comfortable to wear.

Use back stitch to join the thumb, finger, and side seams. Press once stitched in place.

Ruffled Scarf

This lovely knitted scarf is made with garter stitch and short row shaping. Made in chunky mohair, it knits up really quickly and looks fabulous.

~~~~~~

Stitches Used

- Cast on
- Cast off
- Garter stitch

Measurements

17 cm (6¾ in) wide

Tension

36 rows and 22 sts to 10 cm (4 in) of garter st worked on 4 mm (US 6) knitting needles

Materials

100 g (3½ oz) 12-ply (chunky) mohair
Pair of 4 mm (US 6) knitting needles
Wool needle, for sewing up

SCARF

Using 4 mm (US 6) knitting needles and yarn, cast on 30 sts.

Row 1: Knit.

Row 2: K10, turn, knit to end.

Row 3: K5, turn, knit to end.

Rep these 3 rows ending with a Row 1, leaving just enough yarn to cast off.

Cast off. Darn in loose ends.

First published in 2015 by New Holland Publishers Pty Ltd
London • Sydney • Auckland

The Chandlery Unit 009, 50 Westminster Bridge Road, London SE1 7QY, United Kingdom
1/66 Gibbes Street, Chatswood, NSW 2067, Australia
218 Lake Road, Northcote, Auckland, New Zealand

www.newhollandpublishers.com

A record of this book is held at the British Library and the National Library of Australia.

ISBN 9781742575636

Managing Director: Fiona Schultz
Publisher: Diane Ward
Editor: Emma Clegg
Designer: Lorena Susak
Photographs: Natalie Hunfalvay
Proofreader: Simona Hill
Production Director: Olga Dementiev
Printer: Toppan Leefung Printing Ltd

10 9 8 7 6 5 4 3 2 1

Keep up with New Holland Publishers on Facebook
www.facebook.com/NewHollandPublishers

UK £12.99